THE TRAVELS OF PAUL

Adapted by
Etta G. Wilson

Illustrations by
Gary Torrisi

Publications International, Ltd.

After Jesus was taken up to heaven, his disciples went on teaching people about God. Now the disciples were called the apostles of Jesus.

The apostles preached far and wide about Jesus. Many people started to believe in Jesus after they heard the apostles speak. Those who followed Jesus were called believers.

The believers spent much of their time together. They shared their food, clothing, and other belongings. They would often meet to pray together.

There were many believers in the city of Jerusalem. A lot of other people there, however, did not think Jesus was the Son of God. They hunted for the believers and tried to punish them.

One of the people who wanted to catch the believers was Saul. He did not want them to preach about Jesus. Saul went from house to house looking for believers. When he found them, he threw them into jail and threatened to kill them. The believers of Jerusalem were very much afraid of Saul!

One day, Saul heard there were some believers in the city of Damascus. Right away, he went to the head of the religious leaders. He asked for a letter giving him permission to look for believers and to bring them back to Jerusalem as prisoners.

The high priest agreed. So Saul and his helpers left for Damascus. But when he was very near the city, a bright light from the sky flashed around him! The light was so bright that Saul covered his eyes and fell to the ground.

Saul heard a great voice from the sky saying, "Saul, Saul, why are you hurting me?"

Saul answered the voice, "Who is speaking to me?"

"I am Jesus!" the voice said. "When you hurt my believers, you hurt me, also!"

Saul was so afraid that he began to tremble. Jesus spoke again. "Go to Damascus and there you will be told what to do." Then the great light disappeared.

Saul stood up and opened his eyes. But he could not see a thing. Saul was blind!

His helpers led him into the city of Damascus. There, Saul thought much about the words of Jesus and the believers he had harmed. He did not eat or drink for three days and spent the time praying to God.

While Saul prayed, Jesus sent him a vision, telling him that he would be healed by a believer named Ananias.

After three days had passed, Jesus spoke to Ananias, a believer who lived in Damascus. Jesus told Ananias to go to Saul.

Ananias went to the house where Saul was staying. He placed his hands on Saul's eyes and said, "Saul, Jesus has sent me. He will heal you today and will fill you with his Spirit!"

Suddenly something that looked like fish scales fell from Saul's eyes and he could see again! Now Saul was also a believer.

Right away, Saul started preaching about Jesus to anyone who would listen. At the same time, he began to be called Paul.

The religious leaders of Damascus were very angry at Paul. They planned to kill him when he passed through the gate of the city. They sent guards to watch the gate.

But Paul and the believers heard about this plan. After it got dark, the believers lowered Paul over the Damascus city wall in a big basket! And so Paul escaped.

Paul returned to Jerusalem. He wanted to join the believers and the apostles there. But the believers were still afraid of him.

One believer named Barnabas did trust Paul. Barnabas took Paul with him to meet the apostles. He told them what had happened to Paul on the road to Damascus and how Paul had preached about Jesus there.

The apostles were so happy when they understood that Paul was a true believer! Paul stayed with them and began to preach in Jerusalem.

Later, Paul and Barnabas traveled to many distant countries to teach the people about Jesus.

On an island called Paphos, they met the island's governor. A man named Bar-Jesus did not want the governor to become a believer. He tried to stop them from telling the governor about Jesus. But Paul used the power of Jesus to make Bar-Jesus blind.

Paul and Barnabas preached and performed miracles in many other places. And everywhere they went, many people became believers.